MOMOSAS

STERLING EPICURE
New York

An Imprint of Sterling Publishing
387 Park Avenue South
New York, NY 10016

© 2014 by Paul Knorr
Beverage photography by Christopher Bain
Additional stock photography by iStockphoto.com,
Shutterstock.com, and Thinkstock.com

ISBN 978-1-4549-1218-7

Distributed in Canada by Sterling Publishing
c/o Canadian Manda Group, 165 Dufferin Street
Toronto, Ontario, Canada M6K 3H6
Distributed in the United Kingdom by GMC Distribution Services
Castle Place, 166 High Street, Lewes, East Sussex, England BN7 1XU
Distributed in Australia by Capricorn Link (Australia) Pty. Ltd.
P.O. Box 704, Windsor, NSW 2756, Australia

For information about custom editions, special sales, and premium and corporate
purchases, please contact Sterling Special Sales at 800-805-5489 or
specialsales@sterlingpublishing.com.

Manufactured in China

8 10 9 7

www.sterlingpublishing.com

MOMOSAS

FUN ALCOHOL-FREE DRINKS
FOR EXPECTING MOMS

PAUL KNORR

PHOTOGRAPHY BY CHRISTOPHER BAIN

STERLING EPICURE
New York

CONTENTS

INTRODUCTION

When you're pregnant, at some point you will find yourself out with friends at a bar or a restaurant and be the only one not drinking. The fact that you have to stay sober doesn't mean that you have to feel left out. In this book you will find drinks in a range of styles from sophisticated to simple that have flavor, color, and complexity. What they do not have is alcohol. Virgin drinks, alcohol-free cocktails, mocktails—there are many names for drinks that look like they might have alcohol in them but don't. Please enjoy this collection of drinks that are for anyone who prefers to avoid alcohol.

The drinks in this book are organized into six broad categories:
Shrubs: A blast from our Colonial past in which vinegar is used in place of alcohol (they taste great—trust me).

Sweet Blender Drinks: Have blender, will drink. Whether you're blending a healthy fruit smoothie or a decadent ice cream treat, these are the drinks that beat the heat.

Sangrias: A (sober) party in a pitcher. These drinks are great for baby showers and other mostly sober gatherings.

Lemonades: Variations on an American classic.

Fizzes & Sparklers: Bubbles, lots of bubbles.

Mocktails: Alcohol-free versions of well-known drinks as well as some new flavor combinations that will make you forget that there isn't any alcohol.

All are quick and easy to prepare, beautiful to behold, and delicious.

Paul Knorr

TECHNIQUES FOR MAKING DRINKS

Many of the drinks in this book give measurements in equal "parts," as in 1 part this and 2 parts that. This serves several purposes. First, it makes the recipes work even if you're metrically challenged, as there's no need to convert between ounces and centiliters. Listing the proportions also will allow for different-sized glassware, and for making drinks in quantities greater than one—after all, if you're making "mocktails," you're probably among friends, and it's only polite to make more than one at a time. When drinks are more intricate, specific ounce and volume measurements are used. Here are drink-making techniques referred to in the recipes in this book:

Build in the glass with no ice. Add the ingredients to the glass without ice. This is typically called for when the ingredients are already cold and should not be diluted with ice.

Build over ice. Fill the glass with ice and add the ingredients, allowing them to mix naturally.

Build over ice and stir. Fill the glass with ice, add the ingredients, and stir the drink with a stir stick or bar spoon.

Combine all the ingredients in a blender with ice. Blend until smooth. Add ice to the blender and then add all the ingredients. Blend everything until smooth.

Layer in the glass. Pour each of the ingredients into the glass, keeping each ingredient on its own distinct layer. To achieve the layering effect, place a bar spoon upside down against the inner rim of the glass, just above the first ingredient. Gently pour the next ingredient over the back of the spoon to prevent the ingredient from mixing with the previous one. For these types of drinks, the order is important; for best results, pour in the order listed, heavier ingredients first.

Muddling A bartending technique that mashes some ingredients together in the bottom of a glass before adding ice and soda. One famous example of a muddled drink is the mojito. There are special muddling tools sold at restaurant and bar supply stores or online, but all you really need is a long spoon. When muddling, press gently against the fruit or herb to release the natural oils. Don't try to mash it into a pulp.

Shake with ice and strain. Fill the cup or a cocktail or Boston shaker (see definition on page 12) with ice, add the ingredients, and cover it with the lid. Shake it briskly until the outside begins to frost, then take the top lid off (for the cocktail shaker) or remove the pint glass and place the strainer over the cup (for the Boston shaker) and strain the drink into the glass, leaving the ice behind in the shaker.

BARTENDING TOOLS

Even though the drinks in this book are nonalcoholic and there is no need to set up a bar, serving multiple drinks at a party will be a lot easier if you create a staging area and have the right equipment. Here is a list of helpful tools to have on hand.

Bar Mats Also known as spill stops, these mats trap spillage and keep the bar (or drinks area) neat. They are especially handy during messy tasks. Don't forget to wipe down the mats and wash them after each use.

Bar Rags Always keep at least two cloth towels handy to wipe up spills and keep the area clean.

Bar Spoon A small spoon with a very long handle. It has many uses for stirring drinks, of course, but you can use the back of the spoon when layering colorful fruit juices on top of one another. You can also use it to scrape the bottom of the blender.

Blender A heavy-duty, multispeed blender is a good choice.

Garnish Tray Many of the drinks in this book are garnished, so a nice, neat, covered tray to hold your lemon slices, lime wedges, orange wheels, and cherries comes in handy when making "mocktails" for a crowd.

Ice Scoop All commercial establishments require a designated scoop for use with ice, and it's wise to use an ice scoop at home as well. Ice is legally considered a food, so all the food-handling safety procedures apply. Do not use a glass to scoop the ice, or you run the risk of chipping the glass—imagine trying to find a glass chip in an ice bin! Also, keep your hands, used glassware, and any other potentially dirty objects out of contact with the ice.

Jigger A measuring device that consists of two metal cups welded bottom to bottom. One of the cups is usually 1½ ounces and the other is 1 ounce. Some fancier jiggers have handles. Although a jigger is usually used to measure out alcohol, it is a handy device when making drinks that call for one part of this and two parts of that. Simply choose either the 1 ounce jigger or the 1½ ounce jigger to equal one part and you can go from there.

Knife A good sharp knife is essential for cutting fruit for garnish. A knife can also serve as a zester and peeler. It can also be used to cut wedges and slices or to make lemon or lime twists.

Liquor Pours or Spouts There is no reason why repurposed bottles fitted with liquor pours or spouts cannot be used with clear fruit juices and other liquids used in these non-alcoholic drinks. A liquor pour is used to control the flow of liquor from the bottle, and this can help you to measure out ingredients here, too. The pours or spouts help to prevent spilling and splashing and also control under- and over-pouring. Most pours flow at 1 ounce per second; with a little practice and a liquor pour, you can accurately measure an ounce by counting. A "measured pour" has a built-in measurement device and stops the flow after that amount.

Shaker Also called a "cocktail shaker" or "Martini shaker," a shaker has three parts: the cup, the top, and the cap. Place ice in the cup, followed by the liquids; then press the top and the cap on tightly and shake (away from your guests). Hold the top on with a finger to prevent the cap from flying off while shaking. To serve, remove the cap and use the top as a strainer.

Boston Shaker This is a less elegant, but easier, cheaper, and more reliable alternative to the Martini shaker. It consists of a metal cup and a pint glass. Place ice and liquids in the cup, press the glass tightly over the cup to form a seal, shake, and serve. Since a Boston shaker does not have a strainer built in, you will need a separate strainer to hold back the ice as you pour.

Strainer A strainer fits over the top of a Boston shaker or any other glass and is used to strain the ice from a drink after it's been stirred or shaken.

Zester A small metal utensil used for scraping or peeling the zest or peel of a citrus fruit such as a lemon or lime.

GLASSWARE

While a variety of glassware is called for in this book, particular glassware is only specified in certain recipes for those drinks that really should use a particular glass to accommodate volume, offer a particular rim, or show off a pretty garnish. Otherwise, choose any appropriate glassware on hand.

Champagne Flute A tall, narrow glass with a long stem.

Cocktail Glass A stemmed, inverted-triangle-shaped glass. The size varies widely, from 4 to 12 ounces.

Collins Glass A tall, narrow tumbler that holds around 14 ounces.

Coupette Glass Also called a Margarita glass, this stemmed glass is flat and has a wide rim. The most common size is 12 ounces.

Highball Glass A high tumbler glass, typically 8 to 12 ounces in size.

Hurricane Glass A pear-shaped glass, footed or not, reminiscent of traditional Hurricane lamps, usually 10 to 12 ounces in size.

Old Fashioned Glass A short tumbler glass, about 6 to 10 ounces in size.

Parfait glass A tall narrow glass with a thick stem.

White Wine Glass A stemmed glass that varies in shape and size, though typically with a narrower mouth than a red wine glass.

NOTES ON INGREDIENTS

Sugar, Ice Cream, and Juice: The majority of these drinks have one kind of juice or another, and many have sugar, ice cream, or other sweeteners as well. If you are at risk of gestational diabetes or are on a restricted-calorie diet, check with your doctor before trying any of these.

Milk and Cream: There are some drinks in this book that call for milk or cream to be used. In all cases, fat-free, low-fat, or soy milk can be used instead. Some new and interesting flavors can be developed by trying almond milk as well.

Grenadine: Many of these drinks call for the use of grenadine. Grenadine is a sweet red syrup made from pomegranates. Most brands sold in grocery stores do not have any alcohol. It should be noted that some of the brands found behind the bar have small amounts of alcohol in them to act as a preservative. In most cases, the amount of alcohol that this adds to the drink is less than what is found in a nonalcoholic beer. If this is a concern for you, check with your bartender to see if the grenadine contains alcohol.

SIMPLE SYRUP

Simple syrup can be found in some grocery stores next to the grenadine, bitters, and bottled drink mixes. It is also incredibly easy to make at home and can be kept in the refrigerator for up to two to three weeks.

1 PART SUGAR

1 PART WATER

1 Boil the water over medium-high heat. Reduce the heat to low and add the sugar, stirring constantly until the sugar dissolves. Allow to cool and refrigerate in an airtight jar or bottle.

2 Try adding a drop or two per cup of orange, lemon, mint, or vanilla extract to your simple syrup for a subtle flavor addition. A mint-flavored simple syrup would be great in a virgin mojito.

SHRUBS

A shrub is a drink from Colonial times that combines berries, vinegar, and sugar to make a flavorful syrup. The vinegar acted to preserve the fruit in the days before refrigeration. The syrup then was mixed with club soda and ice to make a refreshing warm weather drink.

BASIC SHRUB

1 CUP BERRIES, WASHED AND DRIED

1 CUP VINEGAR (APPLE CIDER, RED WINE,
   OR CHAMPAGNE VINEGAR WORK BEST)

1½ CUPS SUGAR

A WIDE-MOUTH GLASS JAR FOR AGING

1 PINT RESEALABLE GLASS BOTTLE FOR STORAGE

CLUB SODA

1 Wash and dry the berries and add them to a small
   jar or bowl that can be covered. Lightly crush the berries
   with a fork and stir in the vinegar. Cover the jar and store
   it in the refrigerator for a minimum of 24 hours. The longer
   the mixture is allowed to soak, the more flavor the berries
   will impart. Shake or stir the jar periodically to keep the
   contents mixed as they tend to separate.

2 Once you feel it has aged enough (or you can't wait any longer), give it a final stir and strain it into a small saucepan through a kitchen strainer or cheesecloth. Add the sugar and bring the mixture to a boil over medium-low heat, stirring constantly. Continue to boil for a few minutes and remove it from the heat. Let the mixture cool and pour it into a small bottle to store. I used an olive oil bottle with a capped spout. The final shrub can be stored in the refrigerator for up to four weeks.

3 When you're ready to serve the shrub, add a portion to the bottom of a tall glass. Fill the glass with ice and top with club soda.

4 The number of different shrub variations is limited only by your imagination. Different berries, various types of vinegar, and even flavored club sodas all can combine to make a unique drink.

BUBBLY BERRY & ROSEMARY BONANZA

Following the BASIC SHRUB recipe (page 18), use:

1 CUP BLACKBERRIES

1 CUP RED WINE VINEGAR

1 SPRIG FRESH ROSEMARY

1 Combine the berries and vinegar as in the basic shrub recipe. When boiling, add the sprig of rosemary to the pot, removing it before bottling.

2 When serving, garnish each glass with a small sprig of fresh rosemary.

GINGER 'N HONEY REVELATION

2 TBSP. GRATED FRESH GINGER (1 TSP. POWDERED)

¼ CUP APPLE CIDER VINEGAR

¼ CUP HONEY

¼ GALLON COLD WATER

1 LEMON SLICE OR MINT SPRIG

1 Combine ginger, vinegar, and honey in a large bowl or pitcher and whisk until the honey is dissolved.

2 Add the water and stir. Serve over ice with a lemon slice or mint sprig.

GOOD NEWS DELIGHT

Following the BASIC SHRUB recipe (page 18), use:

1 CUP FRESH RASPBERRIES

1 CUP APPLE CIDER VINEGAR

1 TEASPOON VANILLA EXTRACT

When serving, garnish each glass with a single raspberry.

BUBBLE-ICIOUS POMEGRANATES

Following the BASIC SHRUB recipe (page 18), use:

1 CUP POM WONDERFUL®
  OR OTHER POMEGRANATE JUICE

1 CUP CHAMPAGNE VINEGAR

1½ CUPS SUGAR

LIME OR LEMON-LIME CLUB SODA (TO FILL GLASS)

1 Since this uses pomegranate juice instead of fruit, the initial aging of the infusion is not needed. Simply combine a cup of juice, a cup of vinegar, and a cup and a half of sugar in a small saucepan and bring to a boil. Boil for a few minutes and then allow it to cool before bottling.

2 When serving, use lime or lemon-lime club soda instead of plain club soda. You can also try using a lemon-lime soda such as Sprite or 7Up for a sweeter drink.

SWEET BLENDER DRINKS

Many of these recipes say "with ice," as in "blend with ice." This means you should add ice when blending to both thicken and dilute the drink. The amount of ice to add is up to you, depending on how thick and "slushy" you want the drink to be. Start with about ½ to 1 cup of ice and add more if needed.

ALICE IN NAPLAND

2 PARTS PINEAPPLE
  JUICE

2 PARTS ORANGE JUICE

1 PART CREAM

SPLASH GRENADINE

Blend with ice.

THE ONESIE

3 PARTS WHITE GRAPE JUICE

2 PARTS GRAPEFRUIT JUICE

1 PART FRESH LIME JUICE

SPLASH GRENADINE

1 Blend all the ingredients except the grenadine with ice.

2 Pour into a tall glass and top with grenadine.

RATTLE & SHAKE

2 PARTS APRICOT NECTAR

2 PARTS PINEAPPLE JUICE

1 PART FRESH LIME JUICE

Blend with ice.

JUNGLE GYM

2 PARTS PINEAPPLE JUICE

1 PART ORANGE JUICE

1 PART STRAWBERRY PURÉE
  OR SAUCE

1 PART FRESH LIME JUICE

1 PART CREAM OF COCONUT

1 PART PAPAYA JUICE

1 RIPE BANANA

1 MARASCHINO CHERRY

1 PINEAPPLE WEDGE

Blend with ice and serve in a Hurricane glass or another tall glass. This may not be the easiest drink to make, what with the seven ingredients, but it is delicious and great for any kind of tropical or Hawaiian-themed party or shower.

BANANA-LICIOUS

1 CUP STRAWBERRIES
1 BANANA
2 CUPS APPLE JUICE

Blend with ice.

BLUEBERRY BLISS

¼ CUP FRESH
   BLUEBERRIES

½ TBSP. CHOPPED
   PECAN NUTS

2 PARTS RED
   GRAPE JUICE

1 PART CREAM OF
   COCONUT

1 PART PLAIN YOGURT

½ OZ. HONEY

Blend without ice.

BOO-BOO BERRY

1 CUP BLUEBERRIES

1 CUP CLUB SODA

2 TBSP. HONEY

1 TSP. LEMON JUICE

Blend with ice.

BANANA BEAUTY

1 SCOOP VANILLA ICE CREAM

1 SCOOP ORANGE SHERBET

½ RIPE BANANA

1 OZ. MILK

1 OZ. CHOCOLATE SYRUP

1 OZ. STRAWBERRY PURÉE
  OR STRAWBERRY SAUCE

WHIPPED CREAM

1 BANANA SLICE

1 MARASCHINO CHERRY

1 Blend all ingredients.

2 Garnish with whipped cream,
  a banana slice, and a cherry,
  and serve.

BUNDLE
OF BLUE

½ CUP FRESH BLUEBERRIES

½ CUP MILK

1 CUP PINEAPPLE JUICE

PINEAPPLE WEDGE

WHIPPED CREAM

1 Blend with ice.

2 Serve in a tall glass garnished
  with a pineapple wedge and
  whipped cream.

CINDERELLA

3 PARTS PINEAPPLE JUICE

3 PARTS ORANGE JUICE

1 PART CREAM

1 PART GRENADINE

Blend with ice and serve in a Hurricane glass or another large glass.

COCONAPPLE

4 PARTS PINEAPPLE JUICE

1 PART CREAM OF COCONUT

1 PINEAPPLE WEDGE

1 Blend with ice.

2 Serve garnished with a pineapple wedge.

TRIMESTER HIGH

½ CUP VANILLA ICE CREAM

1 CUP MILK

¼ CUP SHREDDED COCONUT

1 TBSP. CHOCOLATE SYRUP

1 TBSP. CHOCOLATE CHIPS OR CHOCOLATE
SHAVINGS

WHIPPED CREAM

1 Blend with ice until smooth.

2 Serve in a tall glass and garnish with whipped cream
and chocolate chips or chocolate shavings.

SWEET CRAVINGS

½ CUP PINEAPPLE CHUNKS

¾ CUP PINEAPPLE JUICE

2 TBSP. SUGAR

1 PEACH, DICED

1 CUP PLAIN YOGURT

1 CUP MILK

1 PINEAPPLE WEDGE

1 Combine pineapple chunks, pineapple juice, sugar, and peach in a blender and blend until smooth.

2 Add the yogurt and milk and blend again until smooth and thick.

3 Garnish with a pineapple wedge.

TIME OUT

2 SCOOPS VANILLA ICE CREAM

2 SCOOPS ORANGE SHERBET

¼ CUP PINEAPPLE JUICE

¼ CUP PIÑA COLADA MIX

2 TBSP. PEACH NECTAR

1 ORANGE SLICE

1 PINEAPPLE WEDGE

1 MARASCHINO CHERRY

Blend until smooth and garnish with a skewer of orange slice, pineapple wedge, and cherry.

HANG TEN

½ CUP CREAM OF COCONUT

½ CUP COCONUT MILK

1 CUP DICED FRESH PINEAPPLE

1 SCOOP ORANGE SHERBET

1 PINEAPPLE WEDGE

1 MARASCHINO CHERRY

1 Blend until smooth.

2 Serve garnished with a pineapple wedge and a cherry.

RATTLE & ROLL

1 SCOOP LIME SHERBET

2 OZ. GINGER ALE

1 OZ. PINEAPPLE JUICE

Shake lightly without adding ice and pour into a chilled glass.

LITTLE NIPPER

2 PARTS ORANGE JUICE

1 PARTS GRAPEFRUIT JUICE

1 BANANA

1 ORANGE WHEEL

1 Blend without ice.

2 Serve in a tropical glass garnished with an orange wheel.

YELLOW BONNET

2 FRESH MANGOS, PEELED AND DICED.

½ CUP CREAM OF COCONUT

½ CUP COCONUT MILK

2 OZ. FRESH LIME JUICE

1 MANGO SLICE

1 LIME WHEEL

1 Blend with ice until smooth, adding more coconut milk and ice if the mixture is too thick.

2 Pour into Hurricane glasses and garnish with mango slice and lime wheel.

MELLOW MAMA

5 OZ. PINEAPPLE JUICE

1 OZ. CREAM OF COCONUT

¼ OF A FRESH HONEYDEW MELON

Blend until smooth. For a completely different color and flavor, this drink can be made with a quarter of a fresh cantaloupe.

PEACHES 'N CREAM

1 CUP FRESH PEACHES, PITTED AND SLICED

½ CUP VANILLA ICE CREAM

1 CUP APPLE JUICE

1 TBSP. LEMON JUICE

1 PINCH CINNAMON

WHIPPED CREAM

1 LEMON WHEEL

1 Blend with ice.

2 Serve in a tall glass garnished with
a lemon wheel and whipped cream.

PEACH LULLABY

1 CUP PEACH NECTAR

2 SCOOPS VANILLA ICE CREAM

½ FRESH PEACH, PITTED AND SLICED

½ CUP FRESH RASPBERRIES

1 Blend on low until smooth.

2 Serve garnished with fresh raspberries.

HOT MAMA

2 SCOOPS VANILLA ICE CREAM
1 CUP BERMUDA STYLE GINGER BEER
1 CUP PINEAPPLE CHUNKS

Blend until smooth and serve. Ginger beer,
like ginger ale, does not contain alcohol.
Ginger beer has a stronger ginger flavor.
Avoid Jamaican style ginger beer in this drink
because it often has capsaicin (the heat in
hot sauce) as an added flavoring.

MINNIE

1 ORANGE, PEELED AND DICED

¾ CUP LIGHT COCONUT MILK

1 TBSP. HONEY

1 TBSP. GROUND FLAXSEED

1 CUP LIGHT VANILLA-FLAVORED YOGURT

Blend with ice.

PINKIE

½ CUP PINK GRAPEFRUIT JUICE

¼ CUP ORANGE JUICE

2 TBSP. LIME JUICE

1 TBSP. GRENADINE

1 LIME WHEEL

1 Blend with ice until smooth.

2 Serve garnished with a lime wheel.

WHOSE MAMA'S BABY?

1 PART CREAM OF COCONUT

1 PART PINEAPPLE JUICE

SPLASH SWEETENED LIME JUICE

1 PINEAPPLE WEDGE

1 MARASCHINO CHERRY

1 Blend until smooth.

2 Serve garnished with a
   pineapple wedge and a cherry.

RASPBERRY RATTLE

1 CUP ORANGE JUICE

½ CUP FRESH RASPBERRIES

1 LEMON, PEELED, SEEDED, AND SLICED

1 LIME, PEELED, SEEDED, AND SLICED

1 LEMON WHEEL

1 Blend with ice until smooth.

2 Serve garnished with raspberries and a lemon wheel.

THE BABY-SITTER

1 CUP RASPBERRIES

2 CUPS WATER

¾ CUP SUGAR

1 CUP FRESH LIME JUICE

Add everything to a blender and purée until smooth. If desired, add ice while blending to make a slushie-style drink.

MAMA-RITA

1 CAN FROZEN LIMEADE
½ CUP ORANGE JUICE
½ CUP LIME JUICE
2 TBSP. SUGAR
½ CUP FROZEN STRAWBERRIES
FRESH BLUEBERRIES

1 White portion: Combine half of the can of limeade, ¼ cup orange juice, ¼ cup lime juice, and 1 tbsp. sugar in a blender with 1 cup of ice and blend until smooth. Transfer the mixture to a container with a lid and place in the freezer for at least one hour.

2 Red portion: Combine remaining half of the can of limeade, strawberries, ¼ cup orange juice, ¼ cup lime juice, and 1 tbsp. sugar in a blender with 1 cup of ice and blend until smooth.

3 Pour red portion into margarita glasses, filling each one halfway.

4 Add a scoop of the frozen white portion to each glass, swirl gently, and top with fresh blueberries.

TICKLE ME PINK

2 CUPS FRESH STRAWBERRIES
    HULLED AND SLICED

1 CUP PINEAPPLE CHUNKS

2 CUPS MILK

1 PINEAPPLE WEDGE

1 Blend until smooth and pour into a
    tropical glass.

2 Serve garnished with a pineapple wedge
    and a strawberry.

PINK BLANKIE

1 CUP FRESH
    STRAWBERRIES, HULLED
    AND SLICED

1 TBSP. HONEY

½ CUP COLD WATER

Blend until smooth.

COOL MAMA

1 PART STRAWBERRY
    PURÉE

1 PART BANANA PURÉE

1 PART COOL WHIP
    WHIPPED TOPPING

Layer in a white wineglass or
parfait glass.

BINKIE PINK

1 MINI SEEDLESS WATERMELON

1 CUP LEMON JUICE

2 CUPS FROZEN STRAWBERRIES

¾ CUP SUGAR

1 Cut the watermelon in half and scoop out the fruit into a blender.

2 Add the lemon juice and strawberries and blend with ice until smooth.

3 Pour into a pitcher to serve.

TROPICAL MAMA

1 BANANA, PEELED AND SLICED

1 KIWI, PEELED AND SLICED

½ CUP MILK

½ CUP PINEAPPLE JUICE

WHIPPED CREAM

1 Set some thin kiwi slices aside for garnish.

2 Blend everything with ice.

3 Serve in a tall glass garnished with a kiwi slice and whipped cream.

MY LITTLE PEACH

1 FRESH PEACH, PEELED, PITTED, AND SLICED

½ CUP FRESH RASPBERRIES

CLUB SODA

1 Blend the peach and raspberries until smooth.

2 Pour over ice in a tall glass and top with club soda.

BABY'S BOTTOM

2 PARTS PEACH PURÉE OR PEACH NECTAR

1 PART FRESH LIME JUICE

1 PART CREAM OF COCONUT

1 TBSP. VANILLA EXTRACT

Blend with ice.

GIVE MAMA
A SMILE

5 OZ. BACARDI®
   PREMIUM MARGARITA MIXER BASE

1 OZ. BANANA SYRUP

2 CUPS ICE

WHIPPED CREAM

1 PINEAPPLE WEDGE

1 MARASCHINO CHERRY

1 Blend the margarita mix, syrup,
   and ice until smooth and pour into a Hurricane glass.

2 Serve garnished with whipped cream, pineapple
   wedge, and cherry.

FRESH AS A MELON

2½ CUPS FRESH WATERMELON, RINDS AND SEEDS REMOVED, DICED

¾ CUP COLD WATER

1 TBSP. FRESH LIME JUICE

1 TSP. GRATED LIME ZEST

2 TBSP. POWDERED SUGAR

1 LIME WHEEL

1 Combine everything in a blender and blend until smooth.

2 Serve in a tall glass over ice and garnish with a lime wheel.

SANGRIAS

To make a convincing sangria without alcohol,
replace the red wine with a mix of brewed
tea for the tannins and cranberry juice
for the color.

ANYTIME-GRIA

3 CUPS BOILING WATER

6 LIPTON GREEN TEA BAGS

4 TBSP. SUGAR

1 APPLE

1 ORANGE

1½ CUPS CRANBERRY—POMEGRANATE JUICE BLEND

1 Pour the boiling water over the tea bags and brew for 1½ minutes.

2 Remove the tea bags and squeeze.

3 Stir in the sugar and allow the tea to cool.

4 Core and slice the apple and slice the orange and place them in a large pitcher.

5 Add the tea and the juice and allow the mixture to chill for at least 2 hours.

6 Serve over ice.

Adapted from a Lipton recipe.

PAPA-GRIA

4 PINTS STRAWBERRIES

6 KIWI FRUITS

1 GALLON RASPBERRY ICED TEA

2 1 LITER BOTTLES SPARKLING WHITE GRAPE JUICE

1 Hull and halve the strawberries and peel and thinly slice the kiwi fruit.

2 Place the strawberries and kiwi in a large punch bowl and add the iced tea.

3 Allow to rest and chill with an ice ring for at least 30 minutes.

4 When ready to serve, add the two bottles of sparkling white grape juice.

5 Serve over ice.

NANA-GRIA

This sangria comes close to the taste of traditional red wine sangria. The black tea provides the tannins that usually are associated with the wine.

2 CUPS FRESHLY BREWED BLACK TEA

2 CUPS POMEGRANATE JUICE

½ CUP ORANGE JUICE

1 ORANGE, SLICED INTO THIN ROUNDS

1 LEMON, SLICED INTO THIN ROUNDS

1 LIME, SLICED INTO THIN ROUNDS

1 APPLE, PEELED AND SLICED INTO SECTIONS

2 CUPS CLUB SODA

1 Combine the tea, pomegranate juice, orange juice, and fruit in a medium-size bowl or pitcher and allow to soak for at least one hour, preferably overnight.

2 Just before serving, add the club soda.

SHOWER-GRIA

4 CUPS WHITE GRAPE JUICE OR ANOTHER
  LIGHT-COLORED JUICE BLEND

½ CUP PINEAPPLE JUICE

2 TBSP. FRESH LIME JUICE

1 LEMON, SLICED INTO THIN ROUNDS

1 LIME, SLICED INTO THIN ROUNDS

12–24 SEEDLESS WHITE GRAPES, SLICED IN HALF

2 CUPS CLUB SODA

1 Combine the grape juice, pineapple juice, lime juice, and
  fruit in a medium-size bowl or pitcher and allow to soak
  for at least one hour and preferably overnight.

2 Just before serving, add the club soda.

FIZZY TEA-GRIA

1 LIME

1 LEMON

1 PART COLD BREWED TEA

1 PART CRAN-RASPBERRY JUICE

1 PART CLUB SODA

½ CUP FRESH RASPBERRIES

1 Cut the lime and lemon into thin slices and place in a pitcher.

2 Add equal parts cold brewed tea, cran-raspberry juice, and club soda. Stir gently and serve over ice.

SANGRI-TEA-A

LEMON-LIME SODA

ICED TEA MIX

2 ORANGES, SLICED INTO ROUNDS

1 LEMON, SLICED INTO ROUNDS

1 Fill a pitcher or punch bowl with lemon-lime soda.

2 Add iced tea powder (1 cup for every 2 liters of soda).

3 Add the sliced fruit and serve right away.

MAMA-GRIA

1 LEMON

1 LIME

1 ORANGE

1 APPLE

1 QUART GRAPE JUICE

1 PINT APPLE JUICE

1 PINT ORANGE JUICE

¼ CUP LEMON JUICE

1 LITER CLUB SODA

1 Cut all the fruit into slices and place in a large (1 gallon) pitcher.

2 Add the grape, orange, apple and lemon juices, and stir. For the best flavor, let this mixture sit in the refrigerator overnight.

3 When ready to serve, add the club soda to fill the pitcher and stir gently.

GRAPE-GRIA

1 16 OZ. BOTTLE DIET GREEN TEA

1½ CUPS WHITE GRAPE JUICE

¼ CUP ORANGE JUICE

1 ORANGE

1 LEMON

1 LIME

1 Cut all the fruit into slices and place in a pitcher.

2 Add the green tea, grape juice, and orange juice and store in the refrigerator for at least 2 hours.

3 Serve over ice.

MINTY-GRIA

1 LEMON

1 LIME

5 STRAWBERRIES

2 CUPS SIMPLE SYRUP

2 DROPS MINT EXTRACT

1 CUP ORANGE JUICE

1 LITER GINGER ALE (CHILLED)

1 Cut all the fruit into slices and place in a pitcher.

2 Add the simple syrup, mint extract, and orange juice and stir to combine. Allow to chill at least 2 hours.

3 When ready to serve, stir in the chilled ginger ale.

LEMONADES

When life gives you lemons, make lemonade,
but only if life also gives you sugar and water.

BLUEBERRY TWINKLE

1 LEAF FRESH BASIL

3 OR 4 FRESH BLUEBERRIES

LEMONADE

1 Tear the basil leaf into small pieces and place in the bottom of a tall glass.

2 Add three or four fresh blueberries and muddle with a muddler or a wooden spoon.

3 Fill the glass with crushed ice and then fill with lemonade.

SINGIN' THE BABY BLUES

1 CUP FRESH OR FROZEN BLUEBERRIES

¼ CUP SUGAR

1 QUART PREPARED LEMONADE

1 LEMON SLICE

1 If using fresh blueberries, freeze the berries for an hour. This will help free up their juice when thawed.

2 In a small saucepan, lightly crush the blueberries with the back of a spoon or a potato masher.

3 Add the sugar and cook over medium-low heat until the sugar dissolves and the resulting syrup starts to bubble. Strain the syrup using a kitchen strainer or a single layer of cheesecloth and let cool. Stir the syrup in with the prepared lemonade and serve.

4 Garnish each glass with two or three whole blueberries and a thin slice of lemon.

CHICAGO CHIC

1 THICK SLICE OF LEMON

SPLASH SIMPLE SYRUP

1 PART LEMON-LIME SODA

1 PART CLUB SODA

1 Muddle the lemon and simple syrup in the bottom of a tall glass with a muddler or the back of a bar spoon.

2 Fill the glass with crushed ice and then fill with equal parts club soda and lemon-lime soda.

3 Stir gently and serve.

HOT AND SPICY

½ GALLON LEMONADE

10 WHOLE CLOVES

5 WHOLE ALLSPICE BERRIES

1 2-INCH-LONG PIECE FRESH GINGER,
   PEELED AND GRATED

1 CINNAMON STICK

1 LEMON SLICE

1 Combine everything into a large pot or kettle and bring
   to a low simmer (do not boil). Allow to simmer for at
   least ten minutes.

2 Remove from heat and allow to cool slightly.

3 Using a kitchen strainer or cheesecloth, strain into
   a heatproof pitcher or carafe.

4 Serve warm with a cinnamon stick and a lemon slice.

THE BUMP

1 CUP BLACKBERRIES

1 CUP RASPBERRIES

1 CUP SUGAR

2 CUPS WATER

ZEST OF 1 LEMON

1 CUP FRESH LEMON JUICE

1 In a food processor or blender, purée the berries until smooth. Strain with a kitchen strainer to remove the seeds.

2 In a medium saucepan, combine the berries with the sugar and 1 cup of water and lemon zest. Bring the mixture to a low boil, stirring constantly until the sugar dissolves and a syrup forms.

3 In a pitcher, combine the berry syrup with the lemon juice and water. Add water and additional sugar to taste.

ORANGE BAND-ADE

2 OZ. LEMON JUICE

1 OZ. SIMPLE SYRUP

1 LEMON SLICE

1 PART ORANGE JUICE

1 PART CLUB SODA

1 Place the lemon juice, the simple syrup, and a slice of lemon in the bottom of a tall glass.

2 Fill the glass with ice and top with equal parts orange juice and club soda.

STORK'S CHOICE

1 PART ORANGE JUICE

1 PART LEMONADE

SPLASH AMARETTO SYRUP OR 1 DROP AMARETTO EXTRACT

SPLASH GRENADINE

1 ORANGE WEDGE

1 LEMON WEDGE

1 MARASCHINO CHERRY

1 Shake with ice and strain over ice into a tall glass.

2 Garnish with an orange wedge, lemon wedge, and cherry spear.

SLEEPY TIME

2 PARTS FRESH LIME JUICE

1 PART PASSION FRUIT NECTAR

2 PARTS SPARKLING MINERAL WATER

POWDERED SUGAR TO TASTE

1 LIME WHEEL

1 Shake all ingredients except the mineral water with ice and strain over ice in a tall glass.

2 Top with mineral water.

3 Garnish with a lime wheel.

POOH BEAR

1 PART LEMONADE
1 PART APPLE JUICE
SPLASH GRENADINE

Shake with ice and strain over ice in a tall glass.

MOTHER GOOSE

1½ LBS. SEEDLESS WATERMELON, SLICED, RIND REMOVED

1 CUP FRESH LEMON JUICE

½ CUP ORANGE BLOSSOM HONEY

1 LEMON WHEEL

1 Purée the watermelon in a food processor or blender until smooth and, using a kitchen strainer, strain into a bowl.

2 Pour the watermelon juice into a large pitcher.

3 In the bowl, whisk the lemon juice and honey until the honey dissolves.

4 Add the lemon/honey mixture to the watermelon juice in the pitcher. Stir in 1½ cups of cold water and refrigerate overnight.

5 Serve in tall glasses over ice and garnish with thinly sliced lemon wheels.

FIZZES & SPARKLERS

Fizzes are simple to make and are a light and refreshing alternative to juice drinks.

THE TICKLE

1 TBSP. RASPBERRY SYRUP

CLEAR CARBONATED SODA
  (LEMON-LIME, CLUB SODA,
  TONIC, OR GINGER ALE)

WHIPPED CREAM

4 BLUEBERRIES

1 Build over ice. Do not stir.

2 Garnish with whipped cream and
  blueberries.

The syrup will stay at the bottom, creating
a patriotic red, white, and blue effect.

DADDY'S GIRL

1 OZ. ORANGE JUICE

1 OZ. LEMON JUICE

2 DASHES ORANGE BITTERS

CLUB SODA (TO FILL GLASS)

1 ORANGE SLICE

1 Shake the orange juice, lemon juice, and bitters with ice and strain over ice in a highball glass.

2 Top with club soda and serve.

3 Garnish with an orange slice.

THE BOUNCING BABY

1 PART APRICOT NECTAR

2 PARTS SPARKLING WHITE GRAPE JUICE

2 PARTS CLUB SODA

Build over ice.

THE NU-NU

1 PART PINEAPPLE JUICE

1 PART GINGER ALE

SPLASH GRENADINE

Build over ice and stir gently for a nice sunset effect.

FRAZZLED MAMA

2 PARTS APPLE JUICE

SPLASH MAPLE SYRUP

1 PART CLUB SODA

1 APPLE SLICE

1 Shake apple juice and syrup with ice
   and strain over ice.

2 Top with club soda.

3 Add apple garnish if desired.

THE SCREAMER

2 CELERY STALKS, CHOPPED

1 TSP. CELERY SEEDS

¼ TSP. CORIANDER SEEDS

1 CUP SEEDLESS WHITE GRAPES

1 CUP WATER

1 LITER CLUB SODA

1 Combine celery stalks, celery seeds, coriander seeds, and grapes in a blender with the water and purée.

2 Strain into a large pitcher or punch bowl using a fine mesh kitchen strainer or cheesecloth.

3 Add the club soda, stir gently, and serve with a celery stalk if desired.

THE PACIFIER

1 QUART ORANGE JUICE

1 QUART CRANBERRY JUICE

1 CUP LEMON JUICE

2 LITERS GINGER ALE

1 ORANGE SLICE

1 LEMON SLICE

1 Chill all the ingredients before combining them in a large punch bowl.

2 Orange and lemon slices can be added for garnish. Also consider making an ice ring using water in a Bundt pan with orange and lemon slices frozen inside.

BABY BOUNCY

1 PART MARASCHINO CHERRY JUICE

1 PART ORANGE JUICE

2 PARTS CLUB SODA

1 ORANGE SLICE

1 Build over ice and stir.

2 Garnish with an orange slice.

COTTON CANDY FIZZ

DASH GRENADINE

SPLASH PINEAPPLE JUICE

CLUB SODA (TO FILL GLASS)

1 PINEAPPLE WEDGE

1 CHERRY SPEAR

1 Fill a tall glass with ice and add a small amount of grenadine and a splash (1 oz. or to taste) of pineapple juice.

2 Fill with club soda and stir.

3 Garnish with a pineapple wedge and cherry spear.

LITTLE MUNCHKIN

2 PARTS CRANBERRY
   JUICE

1 PART GRAPE JUICE

1 PART LEMON-LIME
   SODA

Build over ice and stir.

ROCK-A-BYE BABY

1 PART LEMONADE

1 PART WHITE
   CRANBERRY JUICE

1 PART GINGER BEER

Build over ice and stir.

MAMA'S MO-JO

2 OR 3 FRESH CRANBERRIES

2 FRESH MINT LEAVES, TORN INTO
   SMALL PIECES

1 TBSP. SUGAR

1 TBSP. FRESH LIME JUICE

1 PART COCONUT WATER

1 PART CLUB SODA

1 MINT SPRIG

1 In a tall glass muddle the cranberries, mint, sugar, and lime
  juice with a muddler or the back of a bar spoon.

2 Fill the glass with crushed ice and then add equal parts of
  coconut water and club soda.

3 Stir and garnish with a sprig of mint.

CRAN-RASPBERRY FIZZ

3 TBSP. RASPBERRY
   PURÉE

¼ CUP WHITE
   CRANBERRY JUICE

CLUB SODA

1 Build over ice in a tall
   glass or champagne flute.

2 Garnish with a sprig of
   fresh mint.

If using champagne
flutes, chill all ingredients
beforehand and serve
without ice.

RUBBER DUCKY

1 OZ. KIWI JUICE

1 TBSP. LIME JUICE

1 TBSP. SIMPLE SYRUP

LEMON-LIME SODA (TO
   FILL GLASS)

1 KIWI, PEELED AND
   SLICED, FOR GARNISH

1 Shake all ingredients
   except the soda and
   garnish with ice and strain
   over ice in a highball glass.

2 Fill with lemon-lime soda
   and garnish with a slice
   of kiwi.

EGG CREAM

CHOCOLATE SYRUP TO TASTE

1 PART MILK

1 PART CLUB SODA

Mix the chocolate syrup with the milk to make chocolate milk, then combine with club soda in a highball or Collins glass.

EYE OF THE HURRICANE

2 OZ. PASSION
   FRUIT JUICE

1 OZ. FRESH LIME JUICE

SCHWEPPES BITTER
   LEMON (TO FILL
   GLASS)

Build over ice and stir.

FIZZY APRICOT PUNCH

3 CUPS APRICOT NECTAR

1 LITER GINGER ALE

1 TBSP. LEMON JUICE

Combine all ingredients in a
large pitcher or punch bowl.

PRETTY IN PINK

SPLASH GRAPEFRUIT
  JUICE

SPLASH LIME JUICE

CLUB SODA (TO FILL
  GLASS)

1 LIME WHEEL

1 Build over ice and stir.

2 Garnish with a lime wheel.

TINY BUBBLES

2 PARTS GRAPEFRUIT
  JUICE

1 PART CLUB SODA

SPLASH GRENADINE

1 ORANGE SLICE

CHERRIES FOR SKEWER

1 Build over ice and stir.

2 Garnish with an orange
  slice and a cherry skewer
  and serve with a straw.

BABY SHOWER

1 CUP PARSLEY SPRIGS

1 CUP WATER

½ CUP FRESH LIME JUICE

¼ CUP SUGAR

CLUB SODA (TO FILL GLASS)

1 LIME WHEEL

1 PARSLEY SPRIG

1 Combine all ingredients except the club soda
  in a blender and blend until smooth.

2 Strain through cheesecloth into a small bowl.

3 Pour into glasses over ice, filling each glass about
  a third full.

4 Top each glass with club soda.

5 Garnish each glass with a lime wheel and a parsley sprig.

SMOOTH DELIVERY

1 SCOOP LEMON OR LIME SORBET

TONIC WATER

1 LEMON OR LIME TWIST

1 Place a scoop of sorbet into a cocktail glass and fill with tonic water.

2 Garnish with a lemon or lime twist and serve with a spoon.

MAY BABY

2 OZ. CRANBERRY JUICE

1 TSP. GRENADINE

SPLASH LEMON JUICE

FILL WITH CLUB SODA

1 LEMON WEDGE

1 MARASCHINO CHERRY

1 Shake all ingredients except the club soda with ice and strain over ice in a highball glass.

2 Fill with club soda.

3 Garnish with a lemon wedge and a cherry.

THE TEDDY BEAR

1 TBSP. HOT WATER

1 TBSP. MOLASSES

1 TBSP. LIME JUICE

GINGER ALE

1 In a tall glass, mix the molasses with the water to make a syrup.

2 Add the lime juice and fill the glass with crushed ice.

3 Fill with ginger ale, stir, and serve.

Note: A simple syrup made with molasses (not blackstrap) can be made ahead of time in larger batches by combining equal parts molasses and hot water. The syrup can be kept in the refrigerator for up to a week.

STAR BRIGHT

FRESH PINEAPPLE CHUNKS

1 TBSP. SUGAR (VANILLA-FLAVORED
SUGAR WORKS BEST)

1 TBSP. HONEY

10 OZ. PINEAPPLE JUICE

TONIC WATER

PINEAPPLE WEDGES FOR SPEAR

MARASCHINO CHERRIES FOR SPEAR

1 Place the pineapple chunks in the bottom of a large
cocktail shaker and muddle with a bar spoon or muddler.

2 Add ice, sugar, honey, and pineapple juice.

3 Shake vigorously until chilled and strain over ice
into tall glasses, filling each about half way.

4 Top each glass off with tonic water and garnish
with a pineapple and cherry spear.

PASSION PERFECT

3 OZ. PASSION FRUIT
   JUICE OR NECTAR

SPLASH GRENADINE

SPLASH FRESH LIME
   JUICE

GINGER ALE (TO
   FILL GLASS)

1 Shake all ingredients
  except the ginger ale with
  ice and strain over ice
  in a tall glass filled with
  ice, filling the glass about
  halfway.

2 Fill the rest of the glass
  with ginger ale and serve.

BABY'S KICK

1 PART GRAPE JUICE

1 PART CRANBERRY
   JUICE

1 PART CLUB SODA

Build over ice and stir.

QUICK FIZZY

1 CAN FROZEN WHITE GRAPE JUICE CONCENTRATE

1 2-LITER BOTTLE GINGER ALE

1 In a large pitcher or bowl, combine the frozen juice concentrate and the ginger ale.

2 Stir gently until the frozen concentrate is melted and combined.

PITTER PATTER

1 CAN FROZEN CRAN-RASPBERRY JUICE CONCENTRATE

1 2-LITER BOTTLE LEMON-LIME SODA

1 In a large pitcher or bowl, combine the frozen juice concentrate and the lemon-lime soda.

2 Stir gently until the frozen concentrate is melted and combined.

STILETTO MAMA

2 PARTS PINEAPPLE JUICE

1 PART ORANGE JUICE

SPLASH FRESH LIME JUICE

SPLASH GRENADINE

CLUB SODA (TO FILL GLASS)

1 Shake all ingredients except the club soda with ice and strain over ice in a tall glass, filling the glass about halfway.

2 Fill the rest of the glass with club soda and serve.

PLUSH PUNCH TEA

1 TBSP. SIMPLE SYRUP

1 PART CRANBERRY JUICE

1 PART POMEGRANATE JUICE

1 PART LEMON JUICE

1 PART BREWED CHAMOMILE TEA (COOLED)

1 PART GINGER ALE

ROSEMARY SPRIG

1 Build over ice and stir.

2 Garnish with a sprig of fresh rosemary.

PLAYTIME FOR MAMA

1 OZ. LEMON JUICE

½ OZ. SIMPLE SYRUP

GINGER ALE (TO
   FILL GLASS)

Build over ice and stir.

MR. FROSTY

2 OZ. CRAN-RASPBERRY
   JUICE

1 SCOOP LEMON-LIME
   SHERBET

GINGER ALE (TO
   FILL GLASS)

1 Add cran-raspberry juice
   to a short wide glass such
   as an Old Fashioned or
   highball glass.

2 Add a scoop of lemon,
   lime, or lemon-lime
   sherbet and top with
   ginger ale.

PEA POD

1 46-OZ. CAN PINK GRAPEFRUIT JUICE

1 12-OZ. CAN FROZEN LEMONADE
CONCENTRATE (THAWED)

½ CUP SUGAR

1 ENVELOPE UNSWEETENED STRAWBERRY-FLAVORED
DRINK MIX (KOOL-AID®, FOR EXAMPLE)

2 LITERS GINGER ALE

1 Stir all ingredients except the ginger ale in a freezer-safe
container until the sugar is dissolved.

2 Freeze overnight or until slushy.

3 When ready to serve, if the slush has frozen solid,
allow it to thaw to a slushy consistency.

4 Scoop ½ cup of the slush into a glass and top
with ginger ale.

TEMPER TANTRUM

1 TBSP. SUGAR

1 CUP FRESH STRAWBERRIES, HULLED AND SLICED

1 CUP PINEAPPLE JUICE

CLUB SODA

1 PINEAPPLE WEDGE

1 STRAWBERRY SLICE

1 In a blender, combine the sugar, strawberries, and pineapple juice and blend until smooth.

2 To serve, combine one part of the juice mixture and one part club soda in a tall glass over ice and stir gently.

3 Garnish with a pineapple wedge and a strawberry slice.

TOMATO PATCH

4 OZ. TOMATO JUICE

1 OZ. LEMON JUICE

TONIC WATER (TO FILL GLASS)

1 Shake the tomato juice and lemon juice with ice and strain into a tall glass.

2 Fill with tonic water, stir, and serve.

GOODNIGHT, MR. MOON

1 PART CRANBERRY JUICE

1 PART GRAPE JUICE

1 PART GRAPE SODA

Build over ice.

THE SPANKIN' FIZZ

2 SMALL PIECES OF FRESH WATERMELON, SEEDS AND RIND REMOVED (ABOUT 1 INCH SQUARE EACH)

2 LEAVES FRESH MINT, TORN INTO SMALL PIECES

1 TBSP. SIMPLE SYRUP

1 TBSP. LIME JUICE

CLUB SODA (TO FILL GLASS)

1 WATERMELON WEDGE

1 LIME WHEEL

1 Combine the watermelon, mint, simple syrup, and lime juice in a tall glass and muddle with a muddler or the back of a bar spoon.

2 Fill the glass with crushed ice and then fill with club soda.

3 Garnish with a watermelon wedge and a lime wheel.

GOOD STEPSISTER

1 PART LEMON JUICE

1 PART ORANGE JUICE

1 PART PINEAPPLE JUICE

SPLASH GRENADINE

GINGER ALE (TO
 FILL GLASS)

Build over ice and stir.

ZESTY COOLER

1 OZ. FRESH LIME JUICE

GINGER BEER
 (TO FILL GLASS)

Build over ice and stir.

MOCKTAILS

Here you will find the classic Shirley Temple
and also some alcohol-free versions of well-known
drinks. For the most part, these are new and
interesting drinks that just happen not to have
any alcohol.

APPLE OF MY EYE

4 PARTS APPLE JUICE

1 PART ORANGE JUICE

1 PART PINEAPPLE JUICE

SPLASH LEMON JUICE

FRESH MINT FOR GARNISH

1 Shake all ingredients except mint garnish with ice and strain over ice.

2 Garnish with sprigs of fresh mint.

THE SONOGRAM

1 PART ORANGE JUICE

1 PART GRAPEFRUIT JUICE

2 PARTS APPLE JUICE

1 MARASCHINO CHERRY

1 Stir with ice and strain over ice.

2 Garnish with a maraschino cherry.

DUE DATE

1 PART ICED TEA

1 PART LEMONADE

Build over ice and stir.

Note: *This is a popular nonalcoholic summer drink. Try making a variation using a flavored iced tea such as peach or raspberry or a flavored lemonade or pink lemonade.*

NIGHTY NIGHT

4 OZ. TOMATO JUICE

1 OZ. ORANGE JUICE

½ OZ. LIME JUICE

SALT, PEPPER, HOT SAUCE, AND WORCESTERSHIRE SAUCE TO TASTE

CLUB SODA (TO FILL GLASS)

1 CELERY STALK

1 Build over ice and stir.

2 Garnish with a celery stalk.

PRETTY LADY

2 PARTS LEMON-LIME SODA

1 PART GINGER ALE

SPLASH GRENADINE

Build over ice and stir. This is the same as the Shirley Temple (see page 137) but without the cherry.

Note: You may recognize this attractive drink as the "Brooke Shields," but we think that every mom-to-be is radiant, so we took the liberty of renaming it.

BABY BELLINI

**1 PART CHILLED
 APRICOT NECTAR**

**2 PARTS CHILLED
 SPARKLING APPLE
 JUICE**

Build without ice in a
champagne flute.

BÉBÉ RATTLE

2 PARTS ORANGE JUICE

2 PARTS CRANBERRY JUICE

1 PART GRAPEFRUIT JUICE

1 PART APPLE JUICE

1 ORANGE WHEEL

1 Build over ice in a large Hurricane glass.

2 Garnish with an orange wheel.

JACK & JILL

SPLASH MARASCHINO CHERRY JUICE

SPLASH FRESH LIME JUICE

COLA OR DIET COLA (TO FILL GLASS)

1 LIME WHEEL

1 MARASCHINO CHERRY

1 Build over ice and stir.

2 Garnish with a lime wheel or a maraschino cherry.

Adapted from a recipe by everycollegegirl.com

MONKEY BARS

3 OZ. PINEAPPLE JUICE

2 OZ. LIME JUICE

1 OZ. ORGEAT SYRUP

½ OZ. BLACKBERRY SYRUP

1 Build over ice.

2 Float the blackberry syrup on top.

Note: *Orgeat syrup is an almond-flavored syrup that can be found in some specialty food stores and online.*

PINK BOOTIES

GRENADINE

SPARKLING APPLE CIDER
OR SPARKLING WHITE
GRAPE JUICE

FROZEN RASPBERRIES

1 In a champagne flute,
place a splash (about 1
tbsp. or less) of grenadine
in the bottom.

2 Fill with sparkling apple
cider and float the frozen
raspberries on top.

FIRST STEPS

1 PART COCA-COLA

1 PART LEMONADE

1 PART COLD BLACK TEA

1 Build over ice and stir.

2 Garnish with a lemon
wheel.

MOCKTAILS

SUNNY DISPOSITION

1 PART ORANGE JUICE
1 PART SIMPLE SYRUP
4 PARTS LEMON JUICE

Shake with ice and strain into a cocktail glass.

LITTLE PRINCE

2 PARTS APPLE JUICE
1 PART APRICOT JUICE
1 PART LIME JUICE

Shake with ice and strain over ice into a highball glass.

MAMA'S JOY

1 PART GINGER ALE
1 PART WHITE GRAPE JUICE
1 PART PINEAPPLE JUICE
RASPBERRIES

1 Build over ice and stir.

2 Garnish with a single raspberry. This can also make a great-tasting simple punch. For a punch, garnish with an ice ring with raspberries frozen inside.

PLAY DATE

½ OZ. SIMPLE SYRUP

2 OR 3 MINT LEAVES CHOPPED OR TORN

½ OZ. FRESH LIME JUICE

CLUB SODA (TO FILL GLASS)

1 In a tall glass, combine the simple syrup, mint, and lime juice and muddle using a muddler or the back of a bar spoon.

2 Fill the glass with crushed ice and then fill with club soda.

MULL IT OVER

1 PART POMEGRANATE JUICE

1 PART APPLE CIDER

1 TBSP. MULLING SPICE BLEND PER QUART OF JUICE

1 Combine the juices and heat but do not boil.

2 Place the mulling spices in a spice bag or mulling satchel and allow to soak in the heated juice for at least twenty minutes. If you do not have a mulling spice blend available, the recipe for Cider-ella can be used, substituting ½ gallon of pomegranate juice for half the apple cider.

CIDER-ELLA

20 WHOLE CLOVES

1 LARGE ORANGE

1 GALLON APPLE CIDER

3 CINNAMON STICKS

8 ALLSPICE BERRIES

2-INCH PIECE OF FRESH GINGER,
   PEELED AND SLICED

1 ORANGE TWIST

1 Push the cloves into the orange, spacing them
   evenly around the entire surface. Place the orange in
   the bottom of a large pot and cover with the cider.

2 Wrap two cinnamon sticks, the allspice berries, and
   ginger in cheesecloth tied with a clean cotton string
   to make a spice bag. Place the bag of spices in the pot.
   Heat until the cider starts to steam but not boil. Turn
   the heat to low and simmer for at least twenty minutes
   (longer is better).

3 Remove the spice bag and serve in heatproof mugs
   with a cinnamon stick and an orange twist.

NO RUM FOR RICKEY

1 OZ. LIME JUICE

½ TSP. ANGOSTURA BITTERS

½ TSP. GRENADINE

CLUB SODA (TO FILL GLASS)

1 LIME WHEEL OR LIME TWIST

1 Build over ice and stir.

2 Garnish with a lime wheel
   or a lime twist.

ORANGE AND TONIC
(ATOMIC KITTY CAT)

1 PART ORANGE JUICE
1 PART TONIC WATER

Build over ice in a Collins glass or another tall glass.

THE TIGER'S TAIL

3 PARTS ORANGE JUICE

1 PART LEMON JUICE

Shake with ice and strain into a cocktail glass.

TUMBLE TIME

3 PARTS ORANGE JUICE

1 PART PINEAPPLE JUICE

1 PART CREAM

Shake with ice and strain into a cocktail glass.

PEACHES 'N CREAM

2 PARTS PEACH JUICE

1 PART CREAM

Shake with ice and strain over ice.

PUNCH 'N JUDY

1 PART PINEAPPLE JUICE

1 PART ORANGE JUICE

1 PART LEMON JUICE

SPLASH GRENADINE

1 PINEAPPLE SPEAR

1 LEMON SPEAR

1 ORANGE SPEAR

1 Shake all ingredients except the grenadine with ice and strain over ice.

2 Top with a splash of grenadine.

3 Garnish with pineapple, lemon, and orange spears.

MAMA'S NIGHT OUT

1 PART GRAPEFRUIT JUICE

1 PART APPLE JUICE

DASH GRENADINE

1 APPLE SLICE

1 Shake the grapefruit juice and apple juice with ice and strain into a cocktail glass.

2 Drizzle a dash of grenadine on top for a sunset effect.

3 Serve garnished with an apple slice.

LIGHTS OUT

2 OZ. GRAPEFRUIT JUICE

2 OZ. FRESH LIME JUICE

1 TBSP. SIMPLE SYRUP

SUGAR

1 LIME WHEEL

SPLASH GRENADINE

1 Shake with ice and strain into a sugar-rimmed cocktail glass.

2 Garnish with a lime wheel.

LITTLE SWEETIE

2 PARTS PINEAPPLE JUICE

2 PARTS CREAM

1 PART PURÉED FRESH RASPBERRIES

Shake with ice and strain into a cocktail glass.

THE ROCKING CHAIR

1 PART COLA

SPLASH GRENADINE

1 MARASCHINO CHERRY
  FOR GARNISH

Build over ice and stir. This
is another variation of the
Shirley Temple described on
the next page.

SHIRLEY TEMPLE

2 PARTS LEMON-LIME SODA

1 PART GINGER ALE

SPLASH GRENADINE

1 MARASCHINO CHERRY FOR GARNISH

1 Build over ice and stir.

2 Add a cherry garnish. This is important.
  Without the cherry, the drink would be
  a Brooke Shields.

Note: This is the classic nonalcoholic cocktail.
Legend has it that the drink was invented by a
bartender at Chasen's in Beverly Hills, California,
for the child actress Shirley Temple.

CRANKY BABY

2 PARTS PINEAPPLE JUICE

2 PARTS ORANGE JUICE

1 PART GRAPEFRUIT JUICE

1 PART LIME JUICE

1 PART POMEGRANATE JUICE

1 PART COLA

1 PART LEMON-LIME SODA

SPLASH GRENADINE

1 Combine everything except the sodas and grenadine in a large shaker with ice.

2 Shake and strain into a Hurricane glass or another large glass over ice.

3 Top with equal parts cola and lemon-lime soda and a splash of grenadine.

Note: *This can also be made in large batches as a punch or pitcher drink. Adjust the grenadine to the desired color.*

BUTTERFLY KISS

2 CUPS CRANBERRY JUICE

½ CUP APPLE JUICE

½ CUP POMEGRANATE JUICE

1 CUP CLUB SODA

1 TUBE RED CANDY GEL

1 Combine the juices in a pitcher with ice and stir.

2 Add the club soda and stir once gently.

3 Squeeze the candy gel onto a small shallow saucer and rim the edges of four wine glasses or champagne flutes with the candy, allowing it to drip down the sides.

4 Fill each glass from the pitcher and serve.

Note: Candy gel can be found in some candy stores, especially around Halloween. If you can't find it, gel icing can be substituted and can be found in the cake-decorating section of most grocery stores.

. . . AND EVERYTHING NICE

1 12-OZ. CAN FROZEN PINEAPPLE-BANANA JUICE CONCENTRATE, THAWED

1 10-OZ. CAN FROZEN PEACH DAIQUIRI CONCENTRATE, THAWED

3 CUPS WATER

2 CUPS ORANGE JUICE

2 LITERS CLUB SODA

1 In a large pitcher or punch bowl, combine everything except the club soda. Stir to combine.

2 When ready to serve, gently stir in chilled club soda.

MOCKTAILS

WARM AND COZY

3 PARTS PEAR NECTAR

1 PART CRANBERRY JUICE

SPLASH FRESH LEMON JUICE

1 THIN LEMON SLICE

1 CINNAMON STICK

1 Combine the pear nectar and cranberry juice in a microwave-safe mug and warm in the microwave for thirty to sixty seconds.

2 Add a splash of lemon juice and the lemon slice and stir with a cinnamon stick.

BUMBLE-BEE BLISS

1 PART PINEAPPLE JUICE

1 PART ORANGE JUICE

1 PART LEMON JUICE

Shake with ice and strain into a cocktail glass.

CONVERTING TO METRIC MEASUREMENTS

This chart will prove helpful when converting the measurements in this book to metric measurements:

IMPERIAL	METRIC
1 teaspoon (tsp.)	5 ml (5/1000 of a liter)
¼ cup (2 fluid ounces)	60 ml
½ cup (4 fluid ounces)	120 ml
1 cup	240 ml
1 ounce	28 grams
12 ounces	340 grams
1 pound (16 ounces)	450 grams
1 half-gallon	1.9 liters

INDEX

143